The Ig® Nob Cookbook

Volume 1

Corky White, Gus Rancatore, and Marc Abrahams

illustrations by Marian Parry

© Copyright 2014 Marc Abrahams

Published by Improbable Research, Inc., PO Box 380853, Cambridge, Massachusetts, USA.

ISBN 978-1-939385-16-1

The word "Ig" and the "tumbled thinker" logo are registered trademarks of Improbable Research, Inc.

Contents

Whatzit

Recipes

Whereszit

Foreword
by Marc Abrahams

No matter how many cookbooks you've read, you've not seen one like this cookbook.

The recipes here are all from people who have won Ig Nobel Prizes, or from people who have Nobel Prizes and have gleefuly taken part in some of the Ig Nobel ceremonies to honor the Ig Nobel Prize winners, or from people who helped organize some of the Ig Nobel Prize ceremonies.

Every year since 1991 we have awarded ten new Ig Nobel Prizes. The prizes honor achievements that make people LAUGH, then THINK.

The achievements, and the people who achieved them, are quite real. Most of those people come to the gala Ig Nobel Prize ceremony, where 1100 spectators watch a bunch of Nobel laureates physically hand the Ig Nobel Prizes to the new Ig Nobel Prize winners, with a worldwide audience watching the live webcast. The first four ceremonies where held at MIT (the Massachusetts Institute of Technology), in Cambridge, Massachusetts, USA. The fifth year, we moved two miles down the road, to Harvard University, where the ceremony has happened ever since.

Some of these recipes produce food that's delicious. Other recipes produce food that's intriguing. I wish you bon appetit and happy conversation when you serve them to guests.

Who, you may ask, dunnit? Here's who:

- **Professor Merry "Corky" White** did most of the work of gathering and preparing (in both the culinary and the literary senses) these recipes.

- **Gus Rancatore** contributed wise counsel and gusto-intellectual heavy lifting, and also considerable quantities of Toscanini's Ice Cream.

- **Marian Parry**, illustrator of *The Space Child's Mother Goose*, which properly rearranged the minds of several generations of children who grew up to become good scientists, drew the brilliant Marian Parryish drawings.

- **Geri Sullivan**, master designer of the *Annals of Improbable Research*, designed the book.

- Ig Nobel Literature Prize winner **Glenda Browne**, whose recipe for The The The Thé you will find here, produced the index.

- **Lauren (N.) Maurer Trew** converted everything into the e-book version of the book.

Our greatest thanks, of course, go to the illustrious chefs who contributed the recipes that are about to impinge tastefully on your consciousness.

Corky cooked up the idea of this book, in celebration of the 24th First Annual Ig Nobel Prize ceremony, in the year 2014. Every year we choose a new theme for the ceremony. (The theme does not necessarily apply to any of the new Ig Nobel Prizes awarded that year. Rather, it threads through many other portions of the event, especially the year's new mini-opera, a featured part of the evening.) The theme of the 24th First Annual Ig Nobel Prize ceremony is FOOD. The keynote speaker for the ceremony is Dr. NakaMats, who was awarded an Ig Nobel Prize in 2005 for photographing and retrospectively analyzing every meal he had consumed during a period of 34 years. Dr. NakaMats has contributed a recipe to this book.

You can find more info about the Ig Nobel Prize winners, and the ceremonies, and eversomuch more, at www.improbable.com.

Marc Abrahams is chair of the Ig Nobel Board of Governors. He founded the Ig Nobel Prize ceremony, and serves as its master of ceremonies. He also edits the magazine Annals of Improbable Research *and its web site,* www.improbable.com. *He is a columnist for the British newspaper* The Guardian, *and writes for other publications, as well. Marc's books are somewhat numerous, most recently including* This Is Improbable Too *and its predecessor,* This Is Improbable, *but Marc's favorite among his book titles is food-related:* Der Einfluß von Erdnußbutter auf die Erdrotation, *which translates to the English "The Effect of Peanut Butter on the Rotation of the Earth."*

Introduction

by Merry "Corky" White and Gus Rancatore

We are most delighted to present to you the product of years of research and practice. This is, as the name indicates, an Ig Nobel cookbook. The Ig Nobel Prizes, awarded each year in a gala ceremony at Harvard University, honor achievements that make people LAUGH, then THINK. We have distilled the nutritional essence of the Ig Nobel Prizes into (sometimes) edible form through recipes donated by (1)Ig Nobel Prize winners; (2) Nobel laureates who physically handed the Ig Nobel Prizes to those Ig Nobel Prize winners at the Ig Nobel Prize Ceremonies; and (3) some of we the people who organize the annual Ig Nobel Prize ceremonies.

Food, long considered unworthy of scholarly attention, has come into its own for academic and scientific (and we should add, environmental, political and nutritional) scrutiny. For Ig Nobel attention too, food is a pre-eminently suitable subject – gastronomy that "makes you laugh and then makes you think."

You have evidence in your hands that prize-winning researchers eat, or at least cook, more than packets of instant ramen. The idea that scientists and engineers, innovators and start-up geniuses are successful when they reach ramen self-sufficiency – that is, three packets a day – is a trope among geeks But although ramen itself has become a subject for inquiry (four academic books so far and counting, that we are aware of…) in theeir kitchens and labs, our creators are beyond ramen. Young brain workers are often not about the food – they may even eat their ramen uncooked (dry out of the bag). They pop corn by clustering their smartphones or other electronic devices. They order in pizza in the evening because of its cold excellence as a breakfast food. Everything is washed down (and the dishes, if there are any, are washed) with Mountain Dew, by the romantic light of the Bunsen burner. Their careers if not their guts, prosper.

We have pleaded, begged and bribed these busy people to divulge their Ig Nobel-related food habits and dreams. In these pages, Ig Nobel Prize winners, and Nobel Prize winners who handed out Ig Nobel Prizes to those winners, and also some of the ceremony organizers, have contributed their finest gustatory products. Some (well, one), straight from the lab, have brought us Ehrlenmeyer flasks spewing the mists of liquid nitrogen. Some, more conceptual, have offered theories about tensile strength to be applied, perhaps, to confections of marshmallow fluff. We have examples here of brilliance and of flexibility, of food as technique and precision, or creative and reckless abandon.

Readers and audiences of Ig proceedings will recognize many of the studies producing these recipes: they know for example that herring (probably) communicate through farts. Magnus Wahlberg, one of the scientists who made the herring fart discovery, contributed a recipe for fried herring dinner with mashed potatoes and white sauce which will evoke but not reproduce the original research. Showing the incredible, often edible, range of scientific research lauded by the Prizes, Chris McManus of University College London celebrates his study "Scrotal Asymmetry in Man and in Ancient Sculpture" with a recipe for "Testicles" (quotation marks so no one will think any animal was unmanned for this dish) on Toast. This version is also called "Eggs in the manner of Donkey's Bollocks" and other bawdier titles, but it is, in the end, a testament to the joys of eggs on garlicky toast, with the little tweak of anatomical reference.

Karl Schwarzler won an Ig Nobel Prize for making it possible to rent the entire nation of Lichtenstein (for whatever purpose you might conceive: wedding, tractor pull, product introduction, Quinceanera, or Bar Review Class). His "kasknopfle" briskly introduces the national spaetzle-like dish and reminds us that we too, with enough cash, might some day be Lichtensteinian.

While every attempt has been made to assure that these recipes will work in your home kitchen (or laboratory), we cannot guarantee results. After all, most likely, you the reader have never hat-pinned out thousands of periwinkles from their shells, nor, probably, calibrated the timing of a nuclear oven. Not every reader has access to the dairy products contributed by the happy, named cows near Newcastle University. These recipes are unique offerings, possibly unreproducible, but with your own creative persnicketyness, you can use them to launch your own research, leading (one cannot rule out the possibility) to your own future Ig Nobel laurels. As a former colleague of one of us said often, "Bon Appetit!"

Corky White is professor of anthropology at Boston University, and author of several books on Japan as well as two cookbooks, one of which has just reappeared as Cooking for Crowds: the Fortieth Anniversary Edition *(Princeton University Press 2013). Corky sings in her sleep and in the car. In 2013 the government of Japan conferred upon her the Order of the Rising Sun, Gold Rays with Neck Ribbon, in recognition of her significant contributions to the development of Japanese studies and the introduction of Japanese culture in the United States of America.*

Gus Rancatore is creator and owner of Toscanini's Ice Cream, handily located near MIT, where many budding, and many fully-blossomed, scientists refresh their own genius with his, in the melting shape of bowls of "The World's Best Ice Cream" (New York Times) and "Best of Boston" (Boston Magazine). Both Corky and Gus have helped organize several of the Ig Nobel Prize ceremonies. Gus also created a special ice cream flavor to honor 2007 Ig Nobel Chemistry Prize winner Mayu Yamamoto. (Yamamoto developed a way to extract vanillin — vanilla fragrance and flavoring — from cow dung.) Many other laurels have been placed on Gus' brow for his flavors that make you smile and think, and come back for more.

Igduck, Fried in Butter

by Kees Moeliker, Ig Nobel Prize winner

The 2003 IG NOBEL BIOLOGY PRIZE was awarded to Kees Moeliker, of Natuurhistorisch Museum Rotterdam, the Netherlands, for documenting the first scientifically recorded case of homosexual necrophilia in the mallard duck.

[REFERENCE: "The First Case of Homosexual Necrophilia in the Mallard Anas platyrhynchos *(Aves: Anatidae)" C.W. Moeliker, Deinsea, vol. 8, 2001, pp. 243–7.]*

Although I have studied several aspects of the natural history of ducks, proper preparing of this waterfowl never became part of my home cooking skills. In fact, I only ate duck in restaurants, mostly after an Ig Nobel event.

My highlight of duck eating is on Dead Duck Day. Then, each year on June 5th, at the Natural History Museum Rotterdam, we commemorate the fate of the duck that earned me my Ig Nobel Prize. After a short open-air ceremony, the audience and the now famous taxidermied duck join at the Tai Wu restaurant (Mauritsweg 24, Rotterdam) to savor a six-course duck dinner. This feast includes crispy-fried duck skin in crêpes, Peking duck and roasted duck in lemon sauce.

When Lies Valkenburg, chief cook of The Water Tower restaurant in Rotterdam, invited me to join her to cook a dish of my choice in a professional kitchen, I finally learned a simple way to prepare a duck. I obviously chose mallard (*Anas platyrhynchos*).

C.W. Moeliker

Natuurmuseum Rotterdam

The first case of homosexual necrophilia in the mallard *Anas platyrhynchos* (Aves: Anatidae)

Moeliker, C.W., 2001 - The first case of homosexual necrophilia in the mallard *Anas platyrhynchos* (Aves: Anatidae) - DEINSEA 8: 243-247 [ISSN 0932-9308]. Published 9 November 2001

On 5 June 1995 an adult male mallard (*Anas platyrhynchos*) collided with the glass façade of the Natuurmuseum Rotterdam and died. An other drake mallard raped the corpse almost continuously for 75 minutes. Then the author disturbed the scene and secured the dead duck. Dissection showed that the rape-victim indeed was of the male sex. It is concluded that the mallards were engaged in an 'Attempted Rape Flight' that resulted in the first described case of homosexual necrophilia in the mallard.

Correspondence: C.W. Moeliker, Natuurmuseum Rotterdam, P.O. Box 23452, NL-3001 KL Rotterdam, the Netherlands; e-mail moeliker@nmr.nl

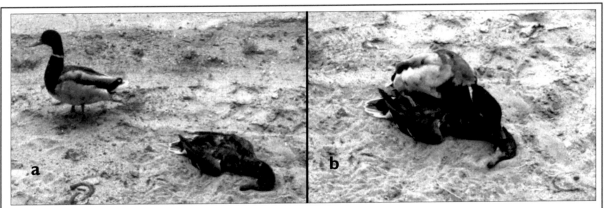

Figure 2 **a** Drake mallard (*Anas platyrhynchos*) in full breeding plumage (left) next to the dead drake mallard (NMR 9997-00232) just after collision with the new wing of the Natuurmuseum Rotterdam; **b** the same couple during copulation, two minutes after photo **a** was taken. [photo: C.W. Moeliker]

Take a complete male specimen from the wild. Ask a hunter or find a specialized shop that sells them.

Do not skin the duck. Pluck it, but do not attempt this yourself. It is a hell of a job. The poultry specialist will immerse the bird in hot wax, cools it and then effortlessly peels the plumage off, similar to the waxing of human body hair. Cut off the head after the skin is clean.

The evisceration should be precise. Take the gut, liver, heart and the like. Keep the stomach. Cut, rinse and cook it for a minute in Calvados. Eat this organ as a snack while working on the rest of the duck.

Loosen the lungs with the thumbs through the neck, and then pull them out. Now the duck is ready for the pan.

Simply fry the duck on the carcass in a small skillet, in lots of butter. I repeat, lots of butter.

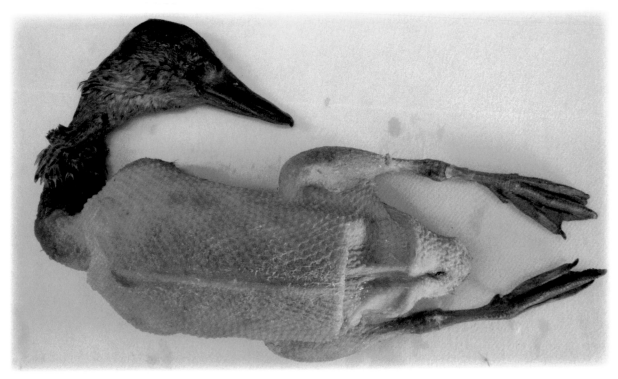

This photo, which shows a freshly plucked drake mallard, all you need to prepare "Igduck in butter," was taken by Willem O. de Jongste, who then consumed a healthy portion of the cooked duck.

Delicious Cake with Cream from Contented, Named Cows

by Catherine Douglas, Ig Nobel Prize winner

The 2009 VETERINARY MEDICINE PRIZE was awarded to Catherine Douglas and Peter Rowlinson of Newcastle University, Newcastle-Upon-Tyne, UK, for showing that cows who have names give more milk than cows that are nameless.

REFERENCE: "Exploring Stock Managers' Perceptions of the Human-Animal Relationship on Dairy Farms and an Association with Milk Production," Catherine Bertenshaw [Douglas] and Peter Rowlinson, Anthrozoos, vol. 22, no. 1, March 2009, pp. 59–69.

Exploring Stock Managers' Perceptions of the Human–Animal Relationship on Dairy Farms and an Association with Milk Production

Catherine Bertenshaw and Peter Rowlinson
School of Agriculture and Rural Development, Newcastle University, UK

*Address for correspondence:
Dr Catherine Bertenshaw,
VETNET LLN North East and
Yorkshire Regional Manager,
School of Agriculture,
Food and Rural Development,
Newcastle University,
Newcastle, NE1 7RU, UK.
E-mail:
catherine.bertenshaw@
ncl.ac.uk*

ABSTRACT A human's attitude towards animals influences their behavior around animals, thus affecting the quality of the human–animal relationship (HAR). Many scientific studies have demonstrated that cattle's fear-response to humans affects their productivity, behavior, and welfare. In the scientific literature thus far it is believed that fear of humans is the predominant relationship on dairy farms. Via a postal questionnaire, we gathered subjective information from 516 stock managers on reported indicators of the HAR and their opinions of the HAR on UK dairy farms. We found that only 21% of farmers believed that dairy cattle were fearful of humans. Respondents accepted that humans can have an impact on

This is my favourite recipe. I have made it "healthier" with whole meal flour and tested my new tweaked version – it is delicious (in all honesty if you are to try it out, the Guinness makes it out of this world, but I prefer the Newcastle Brown Ale as my research was from Newcastle University). The cake pictured here is half quantity.

The Newcastle Chocolate cake (garnished with named cows)

This is an amazing chocolate cake and idiot-proof for even a self-confessed non-baker (my mum baked 10 of these on the morning of my wedding, our friends loved the cake…. I rest my case).

It's good as a treat with a cuppa; as a dessert at a dinner party; without the topping; with ice cream, why you could even have it for breakfast. It also freezes well including the topping.

Cake Ingredients

250 ml Newcastle Brown Ale

250 grams butter (from happy, named cows with access to pasture*)

80 grams cocoa powder

400 grams caster sugar

150 ml sour cream (again from happy, named cows with access to pasture*)

2 free range eggs (preferably where the hens have access to trees*)

1 UK tablespoon vanilla extract

280 grams wholemeal flour

3 UK teaspoons sodium bicarbonate

Cake Instructions

Preheat the oven (gas mark 4/180°C/350°F) grease and line a 23cm cake tin.

Heat the Newcastle Brown Ale in a large saucepan add butter.

When butter melted whisk in the caster sugar and cocoa powder.

Beat together the sour cream, eggs and vanilla essence. Add to the pan.

Whisk in the flour and sodium bicarbonate.

Pour into the prepared cake tin and bake for 45 minutes – 1 hour (if using half quantities: for 30 mins).

Leave to cool in the tin.

Topping Ingredients

300 grams cream cheese (from the aforementioned happy cows*)

180 grams icing sugar

150 ml double cream (as above*)

A few drops of green food colouring (optional)

Small plastic cows for decoration (optional)

*if we use animals, let's give them a good quality of life

Topping Instructions

Beat the cream cheese and icing sugar together.

Beat in the cream.

Mix in a few drops of green food colouring.

Spread on the cooled cake (if you can wait that long)

Arrange the happy, named cows in the pasture

Enjoy with friends. Eat cake responsibly (i.e. in moderation – you will need strong will power)

Best kept in the fridge.

For an even more moreish moister cake, swap Newcastle Brown Ale for stout (one of our local ales e.g. Ouseburn Brewery milk stout, or more readily available globally: Guinness)

Serves 12 indulgent portions – 16 sensible portions

A Bladder-Filling Drink
by Peter J. Snyder and Paul Maruff, Ig Nobel Prize winners

The 2011 IG NOBEL MEDICINE PRIZE was awarded to Mirjam Tuk (of THE NETHERLANDS and the UK), Debra Trampe (of THE NETHERLANDS) and Luk Warlop (of BELGIUM). and jointly to Matthew Lewis, Peter Snyder and Robert Feldman (of the USA), Robert Pietrzak, David Darby, and Paul Maruff (of AUSTRALIA) for demonstrating that people make better decisions about some kinds of things — but worse decisions about other kinds of things, when they have a strong urge to urinate.

REFERENCE: "Inhibitory Spillover: Increased Urination Urgency Facilitates Impulse Control in Unrelated Domains," Mirjam A. Tuk, Debra Trampe and Luk Warlop, Psychological Science, *vol. 22, no. 5, May 2011, pp. 627–33.*

REFERENCE: "The Effect of Acute Increase in Urge to Void on Cognitive Function in Healthy Adults," Matthew S. Lewis, Peter J. Snyder, Robert H. Pietrzak, David Darby, Robert A. Feldman, Paul T. Maruff, Neurology and Urodynamics, *vol. 30, no. 1, January 2011, pp. 183–7.*

The Effect of Acute Increase in Urge to Void on Cognitive Function in Healthy Adults

M.S. Lewis,[1,2] P.J. Snyder,[3,4] R.H. Pietrzak,[1,3] D. Darby,[1,5] R.A. Feldman,[6] and P. Maruff[1,5,*]
[1]CogState Ltd, Melbourne, Australia
[2]Department Aged Psychiatry, Caulfield Hospital, Melbourne, Australia
[3]Department of Psychiatry, Yale University School of Medicine, New Haven, Connecticut
[4]Department of Neurology, Alpert Medical School of Brown University, Providence, Rhode Island
[5]Centre for Neuroscience, University of Melbourne, Melbourne, Australia
[6]Urology Specialists, P.C., Middlebury, Connecticut

Aims: In healthy adults, voluntary inhibition of micturition is associated with an increasing sensation in the urge to void and pain, and acute pain has been associated with transient deterioration in aspects of cognitive function. **Methods:** Eight healthy young adults consumed 250 ml of water every 15 min until they could no longer inhibit voiding. Performance on standardized measures of cognitive function was measured at hourly intervals which were classified as baseline, when individuals reported an increase in the urge to void, a strong increase in the urge to void, an extreme increase in the urge to void and postmicturition. **Results:** Sensations of the urge to void and pain increased with time of inhibition of urge to void and with amount of water consumed. Having an extreme urge to void exerted a large negative effect on attentional and working memory functions (d > 0.8). These cognitive functions returned to normal levels after micturition. **Conclusion:** The magnitude of decline in cognitive function associated with an extreme urge to void was

Our bladder-filling contribution is a drink recipe that hails from Melbourne, Australia, where our Ig Nobel winning research was conducted on the unsuspecting owners of urogenital systems. This drink concoction hails from a basement-level speakeasy, 'The Understudy', on Chapel Street in Melbourne. This recipe capitalizes on the fact that black tea contains sufficient amounts of caffeine to act as a diuretic. Hence, the more you drink, the more you pee, the better you feel!

Instructions

First, infuse a good quality gin (we enjoy Hendrick's, the gin preferred by Queen Elizabeth for her afternoon martinis) with Earl Grey black tea. Allow the tea to steep in the gin for several days to leach out the full flavor and caffeine from the tea.

Next, in a martini shaker mix two shots of the tea-infused gin with a teaspoon of fresh lemon juice and a reasonable amount of coconut cream.

Add one fresh egg white, a few cubes of ice to cool the concoction, close the lid and shake vigorously.

The result is smooth, creamy, frothy and delicious. Your bladder and brain will both thank you.

A Treat to Eat When You Rent Liechtenstein

by Karl Schwärzler, Ig Nobel Prize winner, from the mountains of Liechtenstein

*The 2003 IG NOBEL ECONOMICS PRIZE was award-
ed to Karl Schwärzler and the nation of Liechtenstein,
for making it possible to rent the entire country for cor-
porate conventions, weddings, bar mitzvahs, and other
gatherings.*

REFERENCE: www.xnet.li *and* www.rentastate.com
and www.rentavillage.com.

This is a recipe for "KÄSKNÖPFLE" from Liechtenstein. Easy to do and really tasty. Recipe is for 4 people.

Ingredients

600 gramm Flour

6 eggs

1/4 Liter Milk

2 spoons sunflower oil

2 spoons Butter

1 little spoon salt

3 pinch Pepper

a little bit pepper from the mill

2 pinch Nutmeg

200 g aromatic cheese (Suräkäs) diced

250 g aromatic cheese (Appenzeller) grated

4 big onions cut in stripes

1 small can apple purée

Instructions

Boil a big pot of salted water.

Put flour, eggs, milk, oil, salt, nutmeg and pepper
in a bowl and process it to a dough so it could be
stirred through a riddle with holes of about 1cm.
If the dough is too hard, put some more milk in it
and stirr it until it gets some bubbles. Let it rest for
30 minutes.

Heat up some butter in a pan and roast the onions
until they get dark brown. They should be ready
with the "Knöpfle".

Knöpfle dough has to be stroked through the
riddle and let it cook up until they come to the
surface. Then take them out of the hot water
and put in a bowl layer by layer and always put
the cheese between the layers. When you have
finished, stirr with a wooden spoon. Put some
pepper from the mill over it and top it with the
roasted onions.

Put Käsknöpfle on a plate and serve it with
2 spoons of apple purée on the side.

Enjoy a real Liechtenstein meal with some friends
in a mountain hut. Drink a nice Chardonnay, and
after meal a "Schnaps." Then it tastes best.

Murphy's Toast

by Robert Matthews, Ig Nobel Prize winner

The 1996 IG NOBEL PHYSICS PRIZE: Robert Matthews of Aston University, England, for his studies of Murphy's Law, and especially for demonstrating that toast often falls on the buttered side.

REFERENCE: "Tumbling Toast, Murphy's Law and the Fundamental Constants," European Journal of Physics, vol.16, no.4, July 18, 1995, p. 172–6.

Tumbling toast, Murphy's Law and the fundamental constants

Robert A J Matthews

Department of Applied Mathematics and Computer Science, University of Aston, Birmingham B4 7ET UK†

Received 20 February 1995, in final form 31 March 1995

Abstract. We investigate the dynamics of toast tumbling from a table to the floor. Popular opinion is that the final state is usually butter-side down, and constitutes *prima facie* evidence of Murphy's Law ('If it can go wrong, it will'). The orthodox view, in contrast, is that the phenomenon is

Résumé. Nous examinons la dynamique du toast dans sa chute de la table au plancer. L'avis populaire tient à ce que le toast tombe habituellement côté beurré par terre et que cela constitue le commencement de preuve de la loi de Murphy (loi de la guigne maximum). En revanche, l'avis orthodoxe

My all-time favourite recipe featuring toast is this "Cruzzled" cheese and onion on toast.

Ingredients

2 slices of brown wholemeal bread

100g /4 oz of strong cheddar cheese, grated

1 tbsb of finely chopped spring onion

Recipe #1

1. Preheat the grill to maximum setting

2. Lightly toast the slices of bread

3. Sprinkle grated cheese onto resulting toast

4. Put under the grill and wait for cheese to melt

5. Remove from grill, and sprinkle on chopped spring onion while cheese is still melted.

Now the Ig Nobel twist: Serve either in a large bowl, or on a plate after being cut into roughly 1-inch squares.

In the first case, unless the bowl is very carelessly handled (eg as the result of excess alcohol consumption) the toast will be much less prone to sliding over the edge, teetering on the brink and then breaking into a slow spin – the condition likely to lead to the messy face-down landing made famous in my Ig-winning 1995 European Journal of Physics paper here.

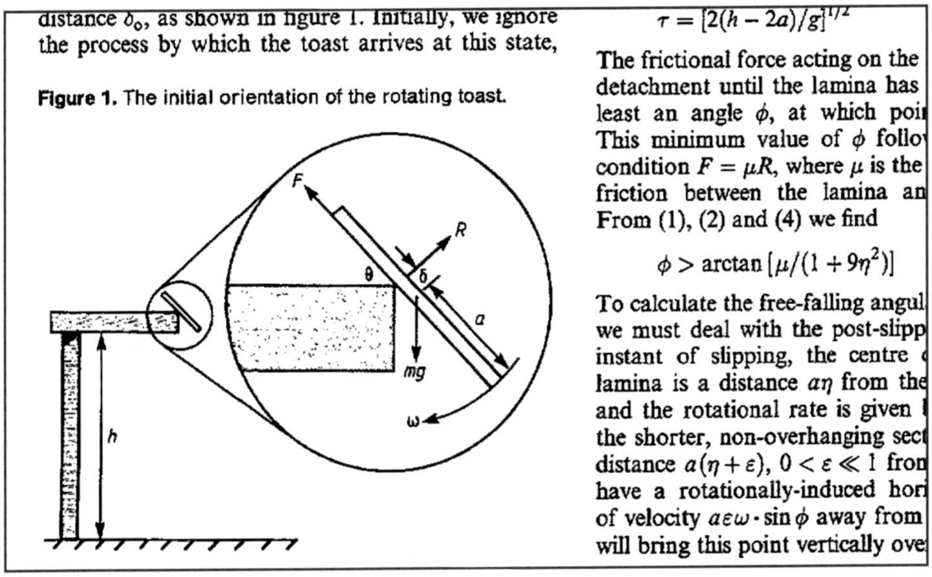

distance δ_0, as shown in figure 1. Initially, we ignore the process by which the toast arrives at this state,

Figure 1. The initial orientation of the rotating toast.

$$\tau = [2(h - 2a)/g]^{1/2}$$

The frictional force acting on the detachment until the lamina has least an angle ϕ, at which poi This minimum value of ϕ follo condition $F = \mu R$, where μ is the friction between the lamina an From (1), (2) and (4) we find

$$\phi > \arctan[\mu/(1 + 9\eta^2)]$$

To calculate the free-falling angul we must deal with the post-slipp instant of slipping, the centre lamina is a distance $a\eta$ from the and the rotational rate is given the shorter, non-overhanging sect distance $a(\eta + \varepsilon)$, $0 < \varepsilon \ll 1$ fro have a rotationally-induced hor of velocity $a\varepsilon\omega \cdot \sin\phi$ away from will bring this point vertically ove

In the second case, again as shown in the above paper, cutting into 1-inch squares leads to a spin-rate so high that there is a better chance of any pieces sliding off the plate landing face-up, and thus (modulo a bit of dusting) remaining edible.

Recipe #2

1. Preheat the grill to its highest setting.

2. Place the toast on a baking sheet and sprinkle over the cheese.

3. Place under the grill and cook for five minutes until the cheese has melted.

4. Serve on a warm plate, sprinkle over the sliced salad onions and the Worcestershire sauce.

Elemental (Liquid-Nitrogen) Ice Cream
by Theodore Gray, Ig Nobel Prize winner

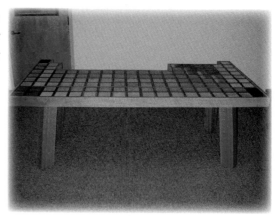

The 2002 IG NOBEL CHEMISTRY PRIZE was awarded to Theodore Gray (USA and Switzerland), for gathering many elements of the periodic table, and assembling them into the form of a four-legged periodic table table.

REFERENCE: http://theodoregray.com/PeriodicTable/

Ingredients

1 Quart Heavy Whipping Cream

1 Quart Half & Half

1 Cup sugar (or 2, what do I care?)

1 Splash of Vanilla

2 Quarts (aprox) liquid nitrogen

Instructions

Combine all ingredients except liquid nitrogen in a large mixing bowl (wood, metal, or plastic, not glass), mix well. Then gently fold the liquid nitrogen into the mix using a long-handled wooden spoon. Mix constantly to avoid over-freezing. Chocolate syrup can be added, but *no alcohol* as this can result in super-cooled liquid causing death or serious injury.

If liquid nitrogen is not available, substitute dry ice flakes created by blowing a CO_2 fire extinguisher into an empty pillow case.

Baked Beans on Toast

by Rich Roberts, 1993 Nobel laureate in physiology or medicine

The Nobel Prize in Physiology or Medicine 1993 was awarded jointly to Richard J. Roberts and Phillip A. Sharp "for their discoveries of split genes." Rich Roberts has particpated in nearly 20 Ig Nobel Prize ceremonies, handing Ig Nobel Prizes to the winners and performing in mini-operas.

Having spent my formative years in England after the Second World War I learned to value simple foods that tasted good, cost very little and weren't rationed. Here is my recipe for the "perfect" baked beans on toast – an ideal dinner after a hard day in the lab.

Instructions

1. Open a small can of Heinz Vegetarian Beans (or just regular Heinz Baked Beans if in the UK or an ex-colony) and place in a saucepan. Simmer at low to moderate heat for 5 minutes, stirring occasionally.

2. Slice 2 pieces of your favorite bread to a thickness of between ⅜ and ½ inch. Insert into an electric toaster and toast until nicely browned on both sides. Do not burn!

3. To the toasted bread, while still hot, apply liberal quantities of a salted butter. Then pour on the beans and add salt and pepper as desired.

4. While eating baked beans on toast I always recommend a good full-bodied Cabernet.

No-Brainer Salmon

by Craig Bennett, George L. Wolford II, and Michael Miller, Ig Nobel Prize winners

The 2102 IG NOBEL NEUROSCIENCE PRIZE was awarded to Craig Bennett, Abigail Baird, Michael Miller, and George Wolford, for demonstrating that brain researchers, by using complicated instruments and simple statistics, can see meaningful brain activity anywhere — even in a dead salmon.

REFERENCE: "Neural Correlates of Interspecies Perspective Taking in the Post-Mortem Atlantic Salmon: An argument for multiple comparisons correction," Craig M. Bennett, Abigail A. Baird, Michael B. Miller, and George L. Wolford, poster, 15th Annual Meeting of the Organization for Human Brain Mapping, San Francisco, CA, June 2009.

REFERENCE: "Neural Correlates of Interspecies Perspective Taking in the Post-Mortem Atlantic Salmon: An Argument For Multiple Comparisons Correction," Craig M. Bennett, Abigail A. Baird, Michael B. Miller, and George L. Wolford, Journal of Serendipitous and Unexpected Results, *vol. 1, no. 1, 2010, pp. 1–5.*

Neural correlates of interspecies perspective taking in the post-mortem Atlantic Salmon: An argument for multiple comparisons correction

Craig M. Bennett[1], Abigail A. Baird[2], Michael B. Miller[1], and George L. Wolford[3]

[1] Psychology Department, University of California Santa Barbara, Santa Barbara, CA; [2] Department of Psychology, Vassar College, Poughkeepsie, NY; [3] Department of Psychological & Brain Sciences, Dartmouth College, Hanover, NH

INTRODUCTION

With the extreme dimensionality of functional neuroimaging data comes extreme risk for false positives. Across the 130,000 voxels in a typical fMRI volume the probability of a false positive is almost certain. Correction for multiple comparisons should be completed with these datasets, but is often ignored by investigators. To illustrate the magnitude of the problem we carried out a real experiment that demonstrates the danger of not correcting for chance properly.

METHODS

Subject. One mature Atlantic Salmon (Salmo salar) participated in the fMRI study. The salmon was approximately 18 inches long, weighed 3.8 lbs, and was not alive at the time of scanning.

Task. The task administered to the salmon involved completing an open-ended mentalizing task. The salmon was shown a series of photographs depicting human individuals in social situations with a specified emotional valence. The salmon was asked to determine what emotion the individual in the photo must have been experiencing.

Design. Stimuli were presented in a block design with each photo presented for 10 seconds followed by 12 seconds of rest. A total of 15 photos were displayed. Total scan time was 5.5 minutes.

GLM RESULTS

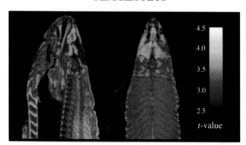

A *t*-contrast was used to test for regions with significant BOLD signal change during the photo condition compared to rest. The parameters for this comparison were $t(131) > 3.15$, p(uncorrected) < 0.001, 3 voxel extent threshold.

Several active voxels were discovered in a cluster located within the salmon's brain cavity (Figure 1, see above). The size of this cluster was 81 mm³ with a cluster-level significance of p = 0.001. Due to the coarse resolution of the echo-planar image acquisition and the relatively small size of the salmon

Here's our favorite salmon recipe. It's real simple except for the 'oven.' The recipe is Craig's (I [George] usually use a TMS machine.)

Ingredients

Some olive oil, a zip-top bag, and a Siemens MAGNETOM Verio 3T MRI scanner (Tim+Dot integrated) with TrueForm magnet and gradient design is all you need to prepare a wildly delicious salmon filet.

Instructions

1. Add one tablespoon of olive oil to the zip-top bag.

2. Add the salmon filet(s) to the zip-top bag

3. Seal the bag, while trying to push as much air out as you can. Place the bag within the head coil in the bore of the scanner.

4. Have the Siemens technician disable the Specific Absorption Ratio (SAR) limitations in software. Other safety measures may need to be disabled as well. You should consult your maintenance representative to ensure that your magnet is properly configured for salmon preparation.

5. At the operator console, when prompted for the patient weight enter 1,000 kg / 2,200 lbs.

6. Scan for 30 minutes, or until the salmon core temperature reaches 47°C / 117°F. Multiple echo, multiple-slice pulse sequences are typically best to create the proper induced heating.

7. Remove the salmon from the bag and garnish as you see fit. Sea salt and a quick squeeze of lemon can be tasty additions.

8. Enjoy!

Romantic, Lovely Torciglione
by Donatella Marazziti, Ig Nobel Prize winner

The 2000 IG NOBEL CHEMISTRY PRIZE was awarded to Donatella Marazziti, Alessandra Rossi, and Giovanni B. Cassano of the University of Pisa, and Hagop S. Akiskal of the University of California (San Diego), for their discovery that, biochemically, romantic love may be indistinguishable from having severe obsessive-compulsive disorder.

REFERENCE: "Alteration of the Platelet Serotonin Transporter in Romantic Love," Donatella Marazziti, H.S. Akiskal, A. Rossi, and G.B. Cassano, Psychological Medicine, vol. 29, no. 3, 1999, pp. 741–5.

Here is my recipe. It is a cake called "TORCIGLIONE" typical of my mother's village, located in Umbria, the central eastern green heart of Italy. It is generally prepared for Christmas and given to friends as a present. It is rooted in a legend saying that in that area in the past there was a ugly dragon that every year wanted a young girl sacrified to it. Fortunately, one day a knight called it. Afterwards, the village people started to prepare the cake, which has a peculiar shape of a snake, and to throw it in the ravine where the dragon used to live.

Ingredients

Almonds without skin: 300 grams

Sugar: 125 grams

Grated peel of one lemon

2 egg whites

Here's a picture of the torciglione.

Instructions

Mince the almonds and put them in the mixer with two spoons of sugar and the lemon peel. Transfer the compound in a bowl and add the rest of the sugar and mix. Whip up the egg whites and add to the compound.

Put it on the table and give it the shape of a small snake, with the neck.

Decorations are very important: use two coffee beans for the eyes, a series of pine nuts (or almonds) along the length of the snake, candied cedar for the tongue.

Put the torciglione on a oven plate covered with oven paper and put it in the oven, pre-heated at 180°C for about 20 minutes, until the surface is golden.

When it's cold put a red flake around the neck of the snake.

Good appetite!

The The The Thé

by Glenda Browne, Ig Nobel Prize winner

The 2007 IG NOBEL LITERATURE PRIZE was awarded to Glenda Browne of Blaxland, Blue Mountains, Australia, for her study of the word "the" — and of the many ways it causes problems for anyone who tries to put things into alphabetical order.

REFERENCE: "The Definite Article: Acknowledging 'The' in Index Entries," Glenda Browne, The Indexer, vol. 22, no. 3 April 2001, pp. 119–22.

Ingredients

4 cups boiling water

4 level teaspoons black thé

3 cinnamon sticks

½ lemon, sliced

Instructions

Put the thé, cinnamon sticks and lemon slices into a bowl. Add the freshly boiled water. Brew for 5 minutes. Strain, put 1 lemon slice in each cup, and serve. Drink while listening to The The.

The definite article: acknowledging 'The' in index entries

Glenda Browne

This article examines rules and practice relating to the filing of 'The' at the beginning of index entries, recommending that the definite article should be accorded more respect, and be considered in filing when the nature of the index entry warrants it.

Happy is the lot of an indexer of Latin, the Slavic languages, Chinese, Japanese, and some other tongues which do not have articles, whether definite or indefinite, initial or otherwise. (Wellisch, 1991: 188)

'The' is an unusual word. It is crucial, and common, yet it is regularly omitted or ignored. What should indexers do about it? How, for example, should we index 'The Who' or 'The Hague' or *The Lion, the Witch and the Wardrobe*?

Based on principles of user expectations, simplicity and consistency, I suggest that we should pay more attention to 'The', acknowledging its role as a significant word. If 'The' exists in a name or title, it should exist in the index entry for

Because of the very high frequency of initial articles in titles of works, it has for a long time been the rule to transpose such articles to the end of the title, preceded by a comma, so that the title can be filed by the (capitalized) word following the article, e.g. *Tempest, The*.

In *Indexes and indexing*, Collison (1972: 198) advises us:

Ignore definite and indefinite articles in arrangement. Omit them where possible; where it is necessary to retain them, invert: *Times, The; Temps, Le*.

The index to his book has an entry 'Bible, The', showing that he felt that 'The' could not be omitted there, even though it

"Testicles" on Toast

by Chris McManus, Ig Nobel Prize winner

The 2002 IG NOBEL MEDICINE PRIZE was awarded to Chris McManus of University College London, for his excruciatingly balanced report, "Scrotal Asymmetry in Man and in Ancient Sculpture." REFERENCE: "Scrotal Asymmetry in Man and in Ancient Sculpture", Chris McManus, Nature, *vol. 259, February 5, 1976, p. 426.*

This recipe is adapted from that wonderful and unusual cookbook entitled *Testicules* by the nominatively determinative French cookery writer Blandine Vié, where it presumably fits somewhere in the sequence of her *Les Cuisines de l'amour, 100 Recettes pour séduire, Les bons petits dejeuners, Premiers repas de bébé, and Les Recettes préférées des enfants.* The English version, *Testicles: Balls in cooking and culture* (trans. Giles MacDonogh, Prospect Books, 2011), has a marvellously honest opening, "Buying Balls in Britain", where it admits "the subject of this book is not the easiest thing to source in the butchers' shops of Britain". The book itself far from consists only of recipes, but also compromises a potpourri of cultural history, animal husbandry, introductory butchery, jokes orchidological, priapic, scrotal and scatological, and a polygot, "lexicon of human testicular terms".

This recipe is a simplified form of "eggs in the manner of donkey's bollocks", and was apparently a favourite of that great bawd, François Rabelais, and is actually oeufs en meurette, eggs in red wine. An etymologically vegan version, albeit on a grander scale, might be possible using what in southern France are called viédases (aubergines; egg plants in North American English), the term derived from vié (penis) and aze (ass, in the asinine, not North American, sense).

Scrotal asymmetry in man and in ancient sculpture

MITTWOCH and Kirk[1] have claimed that "Right and left mammalian gonads do not usually differ noticeably either in

Table 1 Analysis of the scrotal asymmetry of 107 ancient sculptures

		Side of higher testicle			
		Left	Equal	Right	Total
	Left	2	7	32	41
Side of larger	Equal	8	19	17	44
testicle	Right	17	1	4	22
	Total	27	27	53	107

Ingredients *(serves one, but multiply for more)*

Two slices of toast, white or brown

Garlic butter

Red wine (as cheap as possible)

Two eggs (large unless one is unreasonably modest, but duck or goose eggs for those with greater expectations); a pair is of course essential.

Pepper and salt to season

Instructions

Toast the bread, probably done most easily using a toaster;

Spread the toast with the garlic butter, and keep warm;

Add some salt to the wine, bring it to the boil, stir to make a whirlpool in the middle, float in the eggs gently from a cup, and carefully poach for two or three minutes, ensuring that the yolks stay soft, as cutting into them is important for the denouement of the joke;

Remove the eggs with a slotted spoon, hoping that they look anatomically convincing (or at least anatomically ambiguous), and place on the toast;

Serve, preferably with a white wine, and if for guests, with a suitably inventive cover story.

Emerald Bread

by Shinsuke Imai, Ig Nobel Prize winner

The 2013 IG NOBEL CHEMISTRY PRIZE was awarded to Shinsuke Imai, Nobuaki Tsuge, Muneaki Tomotake, Yoshiaki Nagatome, H. Sawada, Toshiyuki Nagata [JAPAN, GERMANY], and Hidehiko Kumgai [JAPAN and GERMANY], for discovering that the biochemical process by which onions make people cry is even more complicated than scientists previously realized.

REFERENCE: "An Onion Enzyme that Makes the Eyes Water," S. Imai, N. Tsuge, M. Tomotake, Y. Nagatome, H. Sawada, T. Nagata and H. Kumagai, Nature, vol. 419, no. 6908, October 2002, p. 685.

An onion enzyme that makes the eyes water

A flavoursome, user-friendly bulb would give no cause for tears when chopped up.

The irritating lachrymatory factor that is released by onions when they are chopped up has been presumed to be produced spontaneously following the action of the enzyme alliinase, which operates in the biochemical pathway that produces the compounds responsible for the onion's characteristic flavour[1-4]. Here we show that this factor is not formed as a by-product of this reaction, but that it is specifically synthesized by a previously undiscovered enzyme, lachrymatory-factor synthase. It may be possible to develop a non-lachrymatory onion that still retains its characteristic flavour and high nutritional value by downregulating the activity of this synthase enzyme.

Previous studies[1-4] indicated that alliinase from any source was the only enzyme needed to produce lachrymatory factor (propanthial S-oxide) from 1-propenyl-L-cysteine sulphoxide (PRENCSO), an important substrate in onion (*Allium cepa*) (Fig. 1a). The reactions from the intermediate sulphenic acid to propanthial S-oxide and thiosulphinate were presumed to be

forming activity could be completely separated from the alliinase activity by passing the crude onion alliinase preparation through a hydroxyapatite column. Further purification of this fraction gave three distinct proteins, whose amino-terminal sequences we determined.

We used the RACE (rapid amplification of complementary DNA ends) technique with degenerate gene-specific primers deduced from one of the amino-terminal sequences to obtain a complete cDNA sequence. The full-length cDNA (GenBank accession no. AB089203) consisted of 737 base pairs, with a predicted gene product of 169 amino acids.

As all of the amino-terminal sequences determined for the three proteins matched the predicted open reading frame of the gene, we assumed that these three proteins were the products of a single gene. DNA-database searches revealed that the gene encoded a new enzyme, which we named lachrymatory-factor synthase.

When we expressed the lachrymatory-factor synthase gene in *Escherichia coli*, the

Figure 2 Don't cry for me: inhibiting the biosynthesis of lachrymatory factor could give rise to a no-more-tears formula for onions.

Ingredients

1 Onion (grated)

1 Garlic (grated)

1 slice of white bread

Instructions

Mix grated onion and grated garlic well at the ratio of 9 to 1.

(You may add seasoning depending on your preference.)

Spread a suitable amount of the mixture evenly on a slice of white bread.

Toast the bread in a toaster oven. The heating condition depends on the toaster.

(I toasted the bread for ten minutes using an 860W toaster oven.)

The mixture on the bread turns green in the toaster oven resulting in "Emerald Bread." Although you may enjoy the color change, I'm not sure if it's palatable.

Additional Information

Either grated garlic (lower left) or grated onion (lower right) doesn't turn green without mixing them. Mixing them is necessary to make "Emerald Bread" (upper).

The reaction scheme of this color formation was proposed in 2006.

The color change like this prompted us to start the research resulting in the discovery of lachrymatory factor synthase (LFS).

Daniel's Chocolate Chip Cookies
by Daniel Rosenberg, Ig Nobel Prize ceremony performer

Daniel Rosenberg prepares the chemistry demonstrations used in classes at Harvard University, and many of the demonstrations that are part of Harvard's Science and Cooking classes and public presentations. He has performed chemistry and physics demonstrations in nearly twenty Ig Nobel Prize ceremonies.

The Harvard course, SPU20 Science and Cooking, and its quantitative approach, inspired me to optimize this recipe. The goal is to make a full bowl of cookie dough, without burning out the mixer motor. The numerical goal: to make the maximum number of cookies in a single batch. The number of eggs is the principle quantum number of the recipe. Divide and normalize accordingly.

Weigh all ingredients on a scale with at least one gram precision. Don't even take out measuring cups. Use nice bowls and tare them on your kitchen scale. Total expected time, half an hour to mix, an hour to rest the dough, and an hour and a half to cook all those cookies.

Ingredients and Instructions

273 g. butter [2.4 quarter pound sticks, cool room temperature of 20°C.]

300 g. white sugar

300 g. dark brown sugar

— Into a bowl mixer of 5 quart capacity, cut the butter in chunks and smash with the flat beater. Add the sugar and cream till fluffy, at least ten and up to fifteen minutes, scraping down at intervals with a silicone spatula. Keep the mixture cool to prevent the foam from breaking, by popping the bowl into the fridge for five minutes half way through. This butter sugar mixture is the foundation of the cookies, so keep on mixing until fluffy and pale cream color.

50 g. dark amber maple syrup

13 g. vanilla extract

— Mix the syrup and extract with a spoon till smooth. Slowly drizzle the syrup down the side of the bowl while continuing to cream the mixture.

3 eggs at room temperature

— Lightly beat the eggs with a fork and drizzle slowly down the side of the bowl. Keep the foamy emulsion cool and again, beat until fluffy.

All of the ingredients are at room temperature to avoid sharp temperature differentials which can break your emulsion. This is the critical step. Careful now.

600 g. all purpose flour

11 g. salt

11 g. baking soda

— Whisk together the dry ingredients before adding them to the wet mixture, about 100 g. at a time, with minimal mixing. Just as the first part of this recipe calls for mixing the ingredients for an unexpectedly long time, the addtion of the dry ingredients must be short and sharp. You didn't spend all that time creaming the butter and sugar to perfection, just to develop the gluten and make tough cookies, did you? Run the mixer by hand, on just long enough to almost mix, scrape down with spatula, add next aliquot, repeat.

320 g. walnuts, broken by hand into chunks about the size of the chocolate chips. No chopping, because it makes too many fine pieces of walnut, which overwhelm the cookie.

440 g. chocolate chips. Get the best chocolate you can, in standard chip size.

— Mix nuts and chips. Add by halves, with minimal mixing. At this point, the mixer will be straining, the bowl close to full. Unhinge the top so the mixer blade can rise up a bit. Again, just a few seconds. A heavy wood spoon replaces the silicone spatula to scrape down and at this point, take out the beater, scrape it off or hand it to a child. If necessary, use the wooden spoon gingerly to better distribute the chips and walnuts, and gently compact the dough. Cover with foil and rest in the fridge for an hour to overnight.

With a square of parchment paper on the kitchen scale, weigh out 20 g. dough and very lightly shape into balls. Don't melt the butter with your hot hands.

Place on an air bake cookie sheet, in a 4 x 4 square grid of cookies. Pack them hexagonally, or tesselate as desired.

Cook one tray at a time in a 375°F / 190°C oven for 8 to 9 minutes. Turn mid-way if your oven is uneven. The last minute goes fast, so don't get all distracted. Conversely, don't be opening the oven to check on them every minute. Pick a time and adjust to taste. Shorter time for pale and moist, longer for brown and crisp. Remove from oven, and let stand several minutes on tray before transfering to a wire rack to cool.

Best served when taken hot from the oven and dropped in liquid nitrogen for ten seconds. Remove from cryogenic bath and eat immediately, to best experience the shell of frozen caramelized cookie surface, encapsulating the gooey warmth of the bulk. Second best, served just cooled but the chocolate chips still warm, with milk.

Best to binge on these babies, as they are the best cookies ever, the day they're made. The day after, they're good but not transcendent.

CANBESMART Curry

by Dr. Yoshiro NakaMats, Ig Nobel Prize winner

The 2005 IG NOBEL NUTRITION PRIZE was awarded to Dr. Yoshiro Nakamats of Tokyo, Japan, for photographing and retrospectively analyzing every meal he has consumed during a period of 34 years (and counting). [See the movie "The Invention of Dr. Nakamats," 2009]

Curry Ingredients

350 grams sword tuna diced

1 tsp turmeric powder

Special Ingredients A:

A pinch red chili powder

1 tsp salt

2 onions sliced

1 clove garlic grated

1 tbsp ginger grated

2 red hot pepper diced

1 tsp coriander powder

1 tsp cumin powder

Special Ingredients B:

½ tsp red chili powder

1 canned tomato

100cc tomato puree

200cc coconut milk

1 tbsp Broth powder

2 bay leaves

Salt To Taste

1 carrot diced

½ broccoli

2 red bell pepper diced

1 package maitake mushroom sliced

250g pumpkin diced

4 small sweet green pepper chopped

½ chopped lotus root

Hemp seed oil as required

3 cups brown rice

Curry Instructions

Cook brown rice with water.

Marinate the fish with **Special Ingredients A** for 15 minutes.

Shallow fry the fish pieces, drain and keep aside.

Heat oil, add sliced onions and stir fry until golden brown.

Add and fry the rest of the vegetables

Add about 1 cup water and **Special Ingredients B**. Bring the gravy to a boil.

Add the diced swardfish and cook for 10 minutes.

Chapati Ingredients

1 cup whole wheat flour

1 tbsp hemp seed oil

About ¾ cup of water

Chapati Instructions

Mix whole wheat flour and hemp oil in a large bowl. Add water little by litte to make a soft dough that is elastic but not sticky.

Divide into small part. Roll each piece into a ball

Heat a skillet over medium heat until hot. On a lightly floured surface, use a floured rolling pin to roll out the balls of dough until very thin like a tortilla. When the pan starts smoking, put a chapati on it. Cook until the underside has brown spots, about 30 seconds, then flip and cook on the other side. Continue with remaining dough.

Serve fish curry over brown rice with chapatti.

Cherry Chocolate Chip Cookies for Mandelbrot

by Deborah M. Geisler, Associate Professor, Department of Communication and Journalism, Suffolk University, and wife of Ig Nobel Prize ceremony photographer Mike Benveniste, whose cousin, Jacques Benveniste, was awarded two Ig Nobel Prizes

Deb Geisler prepared and served these cookies at one of the annual barbeques for Ig Nobel Organizers and friends. They were especially prized there by Benoit Mandelbrot, who invented the mathematical concept of fractals. Professor Mandelbrot participated in several Ig Nobel Prize ceremonies.

"The Mandelbrot Set": Cherry Chocolate Chip Cookies

Ingredients

1 c. butter, softened

1 c. dark brown sugar, packed

½ c. white sugar

2 large eggs

1 tsp. vanilla

1 tsp. almond extract (optional)

2 ½ c. all-purpose flour

1 tsp. salt

1 tsp. baking soda

1 c. dried tart cherries (+ 1 c. hot water + ¼ c. almond liqueur for soaking)

1 12 oz. bag of semi-sweet chocolate chips

Instructions

1. (Pre-heat oven to 350 degrees F.) Coarsely chop the cherries, then put them in a bowl to soak with the water and almond liqueur (I use amaretto). Let soak for ½ hour. Drain, dry off a bit, and set aside.

2. Cream butter and sugars together until light and fluffy. Add the eggs, one at a time, mixing thoroughly. Add vanilla and almond extract. (Almond pairs very well with cherries, intensifying the cherry flavor. Both the almond extract and almond liqueur may be omitted if you do not care for the taste or have allergies.)

3. If you feel compelled, whisk the salt and baking soda together with the flour. Or sift them together. Or do neither of those things, instead opting to add the salt and baking soda to the wet ingredients, mix thoroughly, and then add the flour in 2–3 installments.

4. When the white, dry stuff is incorporated, add the cherries and mix, then the chocolate chips.

5. Drop cookie dough in 1 tablespoon rounds 2" apart on ungreased cookie sheets. Bake for 10-11 minutes. Allow to cool slightly on pans, then transfer to racks to cool completely. Store in air-tight container.

Breakfast for Diamond Makers

by Javier Morales, Ig Nobel Prize winner

The 2009 IG NOBEL CHEMISTRY PRIZE was awarded to Javier Morales, Miguel Apátiga, and Victor M. Castaño of Universidad Nacional Autónoma de México, for creating diamonds from liquid — specifically from tequila.

REFERENCE: "Growth of Diamond Films from Tequila," Javier Morales, Miguel Apatiga and Victor M. Castano, 2008, arXiv:0806.1485. Also published in Reviews on Advanced Materials Science, *vol. 22, no. 1, 2009, pp. 134–8.*

This breakfast is one of my favorites.

Ingredients

2 Eggs

1 Tomato

1 Serrano Chile

Salt to taste

Comestible oil

GROWTH OF DIAMOND FILMS FROM TEQUILA

J. Morales[1,2], L.M. Apátiga[2] and V.M. Castaño[2]

[1]Facultad de Ciencias Físico Matemáticas, Universidad Autónoma de Nuevo León, Av. Universidad S/N, San Nicolás, Nuevo León, México 66450, Mexico
[2]Centro de Física Aplicada y Tecnología Avanzada, Universidad Nacional Autónoma de México, Boulevard Juriquilla 3001, Santiago de Queretaro, Querétaro, México 76230, Mexico

Received: February 19, 2009

Abstract. Diamond thin films were growth using Tequila as precursor by Pulsed Liquid Injection Chemical Vapor Deposition (PLI-CVD) onto both silicon (100) and stainless steel 304 at 850 °C. The diamond films were characterized by Scanning Electron Microscopy (SEM) and Raman spectroscopy. The spherical crystallites (100 to 400 nm) show the characteristic 1332 cm^{-1} Raman band of diamond.

Instructions

Put tomato and serrano chile directly in the flame or grill until black areas appear on the surface of the chile and tomato. Grind the chile and tomato in a blender, in México many people use "Molcajete and Tejolote" is like a mortar until obtain a mix.

On the other hand, in a pan add a little oil or butter and when the oil is hot, add two eggs and whisk, add salt to taste and add the chile and tomato mix.

Serve the mix in an extended plate, serve with refried beans and a slice of avocado. You can eat this breakfast with bread or tortillas (corn or wheat). Remember to take juice and American coffee.

Green Pea Soup (Creme Ninon)

by Johan Pettersson, Ig Nobel Prize winner

The 2012 IG NOBEL CHEMISTRY PRIZE was awarded to Johan Pettersson [SWEDEN and RWANDA] for solving the puzzle of why, in certain houses in the town of Anderslöv, Sweden, people's hair turned green.

This recipe makes enough for six persons.

Ingredients

1 onion

A table spoon of butter

800 grams of frozen GREEN peas

7 dl of bouillon

1,5 dl cream

1 dl champagne/sparkling white wine

Instructions

Peel and chop the onion. Sizzle the onion in butter.

Boil the bouillon and add the onion.

Add the peas and let it boil.

Mix it smooth with a mixer.

Add the cream and let it boil up again.

Add the champagne and add some salt/papper.

Serve at once.

Professor Lipscomb's Tea

by Jean Evans, the merry widow of Professor William Lipscomb, 1976 Nobel laureate in chemistry

Professor Lipscomb performed in nearly twenty Ig Nobel Prize ceremonies, handing Ig Nobel Prizes to the winners and performing in mini-operas.

This is Professor Lipscomb's method for making Tea in the morning.

It was always two cups because he preferred the second.

The evening before, set out:

2 cups on the kitchen counter

1 tin of Earl Grey tea

one snap-together spoon for loose tea

In the morning, prepare the tea as follows:

8:15 am: set out 2 pots of water on the stove to boil.

(The 2 quart Revere Ware is for the 2 cups of tea and the 1 quart pot is for the 7 minute egg which is halved between us, ½ yolk removed from ½ egg for WNL, other ½ egg left complete for JCE. Ideally, 7 minutes leaves the yolk slightly soft.)

Just before the water comes to a boil, pour the first cup of tea and steep for 3 minutes.

Deliver the "first soak" upstairs to bedside of JCE and dash back to first floor within 3 minutes so as to rescue the "second soak" which will have less caffeine the way he likes it. Add a touch of 2% milk.

No sugar.

A Rollercoaster Martini

by Ilja van Beest, Ig Nobel Prize winner

The 2010 IG NOBEL MEDICINE PRIZE was awarded to Simon Rietveld of the University of Amsterdam, The Netherlands, and Ilja van Beest of Tilburg University, The Netherlands, for discovering that symptoms of asthma can be treated with a roller-coaster ride.

REFERENCE: *"Rollercoaster Asthma: When Positive Emotional Stress Interferes with Dyspnea Perception,"* Simon Rietveld and Ilja van Beest, Behaviour Research and Therapy, *vol. 45, 2006, pp. 977–87.*

This is how to prepare a rollercoaster martini:

First of all you need a lot of ice. And I mean a lot.

Then continue with a properly chilled martini glass.

Thus, the real first is actually to put a glass in the freezer where it should stay for at least 1 hour.

Third, get vermouth.

Fourth, get a shaker or pitcher.

Fifth, olives or lemon peel to garnish.

Sixth, gin.

Seventh, get a roller coaster and ride it until the martini is well shaken, but still cold.

Rollercoaster asthma: When positive emotional stress interferes with dyspnea perception ☆

Simon Rietveld[a], Ilja van Beest[b,*]

[a]*Department of Psychology, University of Amsterdam, Amsterdam, The Netherlands*
[b]*Department of Psychology, Leiden University, P.O. Box 9555, 2300 RB, Leiden, The Netherlands*

Received 27 March 2006; received in revised form 13 July 2006; accepted 18 July 2006

Abstract

The current study assessed how negative and positive stress is related to dyspnea perception. The participants were 25 young women with a medical diagnosis of severe asthma, and 15 matched controls. Stress was induced during repeated rollercoaster rides. Results showed that negative emotional stress and blood pressure peaked just before, and positive emotional stress and heart beat peaked immediately after rollercoaster rides. Dyspnea in women with asthma was higher just before than immediately after rollercoaster rides, even in women with asthma with a rollercoaster-evoked reduction in lung function. These results suggest that stressed and highly aroused individuals with chronic asthma tend to perceive

Vivian's Spaghetti Casserole

by Martin Chalfie, 2008 Nobel laureate in chemistry

The The Nobel Prize in Chemistry 2008 was awarded jointly to Osamu Shimomura, Martin Chalfie and Roger Y. Tsien "for the discovery and development of the green fluorescent protein, GFP." Marty Chalfie has particpated in several Ig Nobel Prize ceremonies, handing Ig Nobel Prizes to the winners and performing in mini-operas.

This was the go-to comfort food when I was growing up (1950s and '60s) and my brothers and I still make it. I don't know if my mother created the original recipe or modified a recipe from Foulds spaghetti. In any case, it was terrific.

Vivian's Spaghetti Casserole *(Possibly Modified from a recipe from Foulds Spaghetti)*

1 lb. vermicelli or thin spaghetti

1 large diced onion

½ lb. mushrooms (most sliced, but several caps reserved to dot the top)

butter

2 cans condensed tomato soup

1 soup can amount of milk

½ lb. sharp cheddar cheese

1. Cook vermicelli al dente and drain.

2. At the same time sauté the onions, sliced mushrooms, and caps in butter. Reserve the caps.

3. Heat soup, milk, and cheese until the cheese melts.

4. Mix the onions, sliced mushrooms, and the liquid ingredients and pour over the pasta in a buttered casserole dish. Mix.

5. Place the caps on top of the casserole.

6. Bake at 350° for 45 minutes.

Fartless Herring
by Magnus Wahlberg, Ig Nobel Prize winner

The 2004 IG NOBEL BIOLOGY PRIZE was awarded to Ben Wilson of the University of British Columbia, Lawrence Dill of Simon Fraser University [Canada], Robert Batty of the Scottish Association for Marine Science, Magnus Whalberg of the University of Aarhus [Denmark], and Hakan Westerberg of Sweden's National Board of Fisheries, for showing that herrings apparently communicate by farting.

REFERENCE: "Sounds Produced by Herring (Clupea harengus) *Bubble Release," Magnus Wahlberg and Håkan Westerberg,* Aquatic Living Resources, *vol. 16, 2003, pp. 271–5.*

REFERENCE: "Pacific and Atlantic Herring Produce Burst Pulse Sounds," Ben Wilson, Robert S. Batty and Lawrence M. Dill, Biology Letters, *vol. 271, 2003, pp. S95–S97.*

Here is my favourite recipe for preparing herring:

Instructions

Fry the herring in butter, salt, pepper and parsley.

Make mushed potatoes from fresh potatoes, including pepper, salt, butter and nutmeg.

Make a 'White sauce' (butter, flour, milk) spiced up with parsley, lemon and salt.

Delicious :)

Sounds produced by herring (*Clupea harengus*) bubble release

Magnus Wahlberg [*,1], Håkan Westerberg

Institute of Coastal Research, National Board of Fisheries, Sweden

Accepted 19 December 2002

Abstract

In the herring (*Clupea harengus*), the swim bladder is connected to both the alimentary canal and the anal opening. The anterior duct is used for filling the swim bladder with air. Gas release from the anal opening is often observed when the fish is scared or during ascent and descent. Here, the sounds produced by such a gas release are studied. The fish was kept in a low-pressure chamber. As the ambient pressure was reduced, the gas in the swim bladder expanded and was emitted through the anal opening. Herring sounds were also recorded in a fish trap and in the field. The characteristic sound made by herring during gas release is denoted as the pulsed chirp. This pulsed chirp is 32–133 ms long ($N = 11$) and consists of a series of 7–50 ($N = 11$) transient pulses with a continuous reduction of the frequency emphasis (centroid frequency of first pulse 4.1 kHz and of last pulse 3.0 kHz, $N = 11$). The source level of the chirp is 73 ± 8 dB re 1 μPa rms (root mean square) at 1 m ($N = 19$). The pulsed chirp is not known to be produced by any other marine animal and may be a good fingerprint for identifying schools of clupeid fish by natural predators, fishery scientists and fishermen. A model for the generation of the pulsed chirp is presented and tested on existing data.

© 2003 Éditions scientifiques et médicales Elsevier SAS and Ifremer/IRD/Inra/Cemagref. All rights reserved.

Keywords: Bioacoustics; Sound production; Gas release; Herring

1. Introduction

The herring (*Clupea harengus*) is quantitatively the most important fish species of northern Europe. During decades of intense research, we have learned about its migratory, diurnal and foraging behavior, and about its role in the marine food web (Klinkhardt, 1996). In spite of this, little is known about herring sound production and communication. In this study, we focus on acoustic signals produced by herring.

Compared to most other fish species, herring has excellent hearing abilities (Enger, 1967). In clupeid fish, the swim

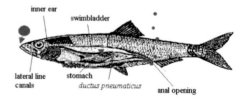

Fig. 1. The airways of herring (*Clupea harengus*). Redrawn from Klinkhardt (1996). The assumed path of air (see text) is indicated with gray circles and arrows.

Index

18880413R00024

Made in the USA
Middletown, DE
02 December 2018